FAMILY BUSINESS GOVERNANCE

MAXIMIZING FAMILY AND BUSINESS POTENTIAL

by
Craig E. Aronoff, Ph.D.
John L. Ward, Ph.D.

*Family Business
Leadership Series, No. 8*

Business Owner Resources
P.O. Box 4356
Marietta, Georgia 30061-4356

ISSN: 1071-5010
ISBN: 0-9651011-8-5
©1996
Second Printing

Family Business Leadership Series

We believe that family businesses are special, not only to the families that own and manage them but to our society and to the private enterprise system. Having worked and interacted with hundreds of family enterprises in the past twenty years, we offer the insights of that experience and the collected wisdom of the best and most successful family firms in North America.

This volume is a part of a series offering practical guidance for family businesses seeking to manage the special challenges and opportunities confronting them.

To order additional copies, contact:
Business Owner Resources
Post Office Box 4356
Marietta, Georgia 30061-4356
Tel: 1-800-551-0633

Quantity discounts are available.

Individual volume price: $14.95

Other volumes in the series include:

Family Business Succession: The Final Test of Greatness

Family Meetings: How to Build a Stronger Family and a Stronger Business

Another Kind of Hero: Preparing Successors for Leadership

How Families Work Together

Family Business Compensation

How To Choose & Use Advisors: Getting the Best Professional Family Business Advice

Financing Transitions: Handling Capital & Liquidity in the Family Business

Preparing Your Family Business for Strategic Change

Contents

Tables and Exhibits

I. Introduction

■

govern — the aim of keeping in a straight course or smooth operation for the good of the individual and the whole.

—Webster's Dictionary

■

Family business leaders seldom think of themselves as "governing" the business or the family.

Yet thoughtful business owners almost universally value **the goals of good governance**, both in the business and the family — peace, cohesiveness, effective conflict resolution and freedom from internecine political warfare to pursue shared objectives and values.

A business that is well-governed is free to work toward the highest and best objectives of business — maximizing profit, improving strategy, creating jobs, fostering employee development and serving all stakeholders, including shareholders, employees, customers, suppliers and the community.

And while most people do not think of "governance" in a family context, **a family that runs smoothly is free to nurture and expand upon the most positive elements of its heritage**, such as family values, pride, unity, history, tradition, mutual support and legacies of service.

Families in business together have an especially powerful motivation to govern themselves well. They hold shared interests that are vast and profound, often including a large capital investment, prospects for future employment of themselves and their offspring, and the larger-than-life image of a family business in its community.

Many business-owning families drift unconsciously into haphazard or destructive patterns of decisionmaking and communicating that can threaten and even destroy those shared interests.

1

Yet many business-owning families drift unconsciously into haphazard or destructive patterns of decisionmaking and communicating that can threaten and even destroy those shared interests.

Binding together for the general good. After its stormy Atlantic crossing in the year 1620, the day the Mayflower anchored off Cape Cod, Massachusetts, 41 adults aboard came together and signed the Mayflower Compact. Drawing upon what historians Samuel Morison and Henry Steele Commager have called "a remarkable instinct for self-government," they agreed to a code that would bind them together for the general good of their proposed colony. Though their agreement lacked legal status, it had the strength of common consent and became a benchmark for governing institutions worldwide.

Similarly, a desire to work together for the general good of the family and the business is the common glue a growing number of family business owners are using to establish a framework for governance — the principles and processes that enable maximization of the potential of both the family and the business. In this way, families can draw upon the same strength of common consent recognized by the Pilgrims to fuel productive growth in their businesses and forge a unified and committed family — goals few business owners would disagree with.

Purpose of this booklet. Our purpose here is to describe principles and processes of effective family business governance. This booklet explains the importance of maintaining two distinct points of focus — the family and the business. It lays out governance processes for organizing each of these two equally important domains: family meetings or a family council for family concerns; and an active board of directors, preferably including a majority of independent board members, for the business.

The booklet lays out the distinct functions of family and business and areas in which they overlap. It offers specific techniques for smoothing communication between the family and the board. And, to aid future planning, the booklet shows how business and family governance processes typically change as the business evolves from its entrepreneurial stage to later generations of family ownership.

In the process, the booklet will show **how effective governance can empower leaders of the business and the family to make the most of the unique strength of family business: The synergy between a strong, unified owning family and a well-run family enterprise.**

II. The Importance of Thoughtful and Effective Governance

The history of family business is full of ruinous examples of what can happen in the absence of effective governance.

Emotions among even a handful of shareholders can erupt into clashes that disrupt strategic planning, tie up management in court for years and drain corporate assets. The Posner family, the Schoens of U-Haul, the Robbies of the Miami Dolphins, and the Haft family, owners of the Dart retailing empire, are well-known examples.

In another extreme example, a second-generation minority shareholder in a family business was denied any information about the performance of her investment. She was refused the opportunity to work in the business. Her attempts to redeem her shares were summarily rebuffed and her requests for higher dividends were refused. Her petition for a board seat was denied.

The result: Her relationship with the other two shareholders, her brothers, had crumbled into enduring bitterness. In frustration, the sister decided to use either litigation or a damaging media campaign against her brothers to escape from what had become a costly burden — family business ownership.

How could effective governance processes have averted this problem? First, **effective governance requires accountability between shareholders and the business**. If the founder of this business had begun family meetings to teach these principles in the first generation of family ownership, his three children might have learned accountability — a value that would have prevented his sons as adults from behaving in a way that rendered their sister's shares worthless to her.

Second, **effective governance requires setting family policies that would have prevented the seemingly arbitrary decisions that the sister found so damaging**. Such policies govern family members' participation in the business, liquidity for shareholders, information and education for shareholders, responsible stewardship of shareholders' assets, family succession on the board and other potentially contentious matters. Policies and procedures, once accepted and understood, provide for shared expectations and a sense of consistency and fairness.

Just as successful societies embrace a rule of law, smooth-running family businesses embrace policies that provide for orderly decision-making on difficult issues. Through the governance process, family

3

Effective governance can be defined as creating processes that make revolution unnecessary.

members define fairness relative to necessary sacrifices as well as distribution of benefits. In a way, effective governance can be defined as creating processes that make revolution unnecessary. In the absence of these processes, as the example of the alienated sister shows, shareholders' needs denied do not go away; they fester and turn malignant.

The importance of accountability. It is easy to resist accountability in the family firm. A business may survive and thrive temporarily on the energy, vision and knowledge of a fiercely independent, high-achieving founder. He or she may hold employees and family members accountable, but may see no particular need for developing an organized approach to accountability.

But because no one lives forever, the lifeline provided by the single strong leader inevitably snaps. Then, the business and the family both can fall victim to a profound and urgent need for governance processes that protect the interests of both family and business.

Three dimensions of governance are intrinsic to any family business, and each must be accountable to the other two. (Please see Exhibit 1.) Most obvious is day-to-day management of business concerns — running operations, finance, employees, supplier and customer relationships and so on. These are the responsibilities of management. They are the domain of the chief executive or executive committee and are not a focus of this booklet.

The remaining two domains of governance are our focus here. Ownership or shareholder concerns encompass:

- liquidity issues;
- allocation of corporate capital;
- the survival of the business through ownership and management succession;
- the performance of shareholders' investment;
- strategic direction; and the like.

Family concerns are an equally important, but more often neglected dimension of family business governance. These encompass:

- family members' shared interests in the health, prosperity and continuity of the family;
- family participation in the business;

4

- the role and image of the business in the community;
- information and education of family members;
- family communication;
- manifesting family values and goals in the business; and more.

EXHIBIT 1

Dimensions of Family Business Governance

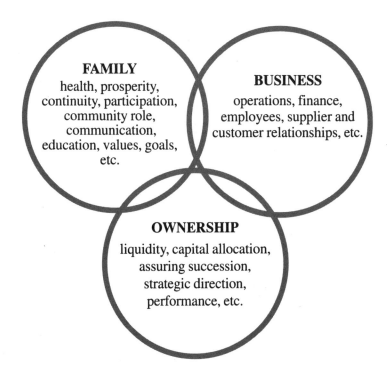

FAMILY
health, prosperity, continuity, participation, community role, communication, education, values, goals, etc.

BUSINESS
operations, finance, employees, supplier and customer relationships, etc.

OWNERSHIP
liquidity, capital allocation, assuring succession, strategic direction, performance, etc.

Each of these governance dimensions warrants special attention. Each has tremendous potential as a positive force in the family business.

And if neglected, each has vast destructive power. Consider these fictitious examples:

—For estate-planning purposes, four siblings who are third-generation owners of ABC Co., a family business, are given ownership of a newly acquired subsidiary of the family business. When one brother develops serious personal financial problems, the siblings agree, without talking to other family members, to take a large amount of cash out of the business — enough for the troubled brother to stave off bankruptcy and for each of the remaining siblings to feel they have been "fairly treated." But the distribution seriously weakens the subsidiary, forces the parent company to rush to the rescue with an unplanned cash infusion (depleting its R&D funds) and angers senior family members.

—A second-generation family business CEO, son of the founder, pursues an aggressive growth strategy for the family business, XYZ Co., pumping cash into acquisitions. The value of the business is increasing rapidly on paper, but shareholder dividends remain low. Family members, kept in the dark about the business's financial performance, are increasingly vocal and pointed in their criticism of the CEO. He, meanwhile, grows angry when a trusted professional advisor to the company urges him to delay plans to increase his bonus. "I'm making my relatives rich. What's their problem?" the CEO complains.

—The third-generation CEO of Thunderhead Corp., a family business, is clearly grooming as a successor his protege, a nonfamily Ivy League MBA who has successfully overhauled the business's financial-reporting systems. But several other family members among the business's 14 shareholders discover while chatting at a family gathering that they share strong feelings in favor of continuing leadership of the business by a family member. When they approach the CEO, he brushes them off, reasoning that "they don't understand the business issues" behind his choice. Angry, the dissatisfied shareholders, several of whom hold seats on the board, start planning to organize a board majority in opposition to the CEO's choice.

While these three dilemmas could be dismissed as the result of such "human failings" as poor communication or bad judgment, the root cause is actually a failure of family business governance. In each case, decision-makers failed to hold themselves accountable. Regardless of the merits of their decisions, the consequences of that failure became a stumbling block.

In the case of ABC Co., the three siblings attended to family concerns without holding themselves accountable to the business.

In the case of XYZ Co., the CEO is pursuing his strategy for the business without holding himself accountable to shareholders.

At Thunderhead Corp., the third example, the CEO is attending to business interests without holding himself accountable to family goals relating to family business leadership.

Accountability in family business governance doesn't mean turning the business into a democracy or "giving away the store." It merely means setting up processes that ensure respect for the interests of both the business and the family.

Business First? Or Family First? Another stumbling block for family business leaders is the assumption that they must choose one set of interests over another — embracing a "family first" or "business first" philosophy of governance.

Some business leaders put "family first" and operate on the premise that family members have a *right* to be heard under any circumstances — no matter how disruptive to the business their self-expression may be. They proceed on the assumption that family members' ideas always should be taken seriously and that business leaders should report back to the family. In this line of thinking, the business should compromise to avoid potential family conflict and assure family harmony.

Over time, either a "business first" or "family first" mode of operation can cause serious problems. A "business first" perspective allows family concerns to fester and erupt into clashes that can threaten the future of the business. A "family first" view can distract and drain management and undermine the competitiveness of the business. Either sharply increases the likelihood of conflict between managers and shareholders.

Other family business leaders put "business first." They discriminate against family members who lack skill, knowledge and proven experience. They assume some family members' comments on the business are always inappropriate and disrupt management. In this line of thinking, shareholders should be passive. Over time, either a "business first" or "family first" mode of operation can cause serious problems. A "business first" perspective allows family concerns to fester and erupt into clashes that can threaten the future of the business. A "family first" view can distract and drain management and undermine the competitiveness of the business. Either sharply increases the likelihood of conflict between managers and shareholders.

In fact, both family and business domains are crucial to long-term family business prosperity. Both require equal care. Neither needs to assume a dominant role. Instead, respect for the needs of the business must be balanced with legitimate family concerns if the family business — and the family — are to endure. Appropriate governance can provide balance responsive to all.

The special role of the family. The importance of good governance of the business is often evident to the experienced business owner, who understands the need for perspective, accountability and breadth of resources in making business decisions.

The importance of family governance is not always as obvious. But in fact, **one of the greatest values of owning a family business is the opportunity it provides the family to experience the rewards of coming together and working together on common interests and goals.**

The dynamic quality of a cohesive, conscientious family bears powerful reciprocal benefits to the business, conveying a positive message to all stakeholders. Consensus-building efforts by the family show that the family feels a sense of responsibility to all those connected with the business. That message to employees, customers, suppliers and the community at large builds confidence in the business and its future.

The risks of neglecting the family. But without governance processes that systematically encourage families to attend to shared concerns, most families find the business becomes too central a focus in everyone's thinking.

Too often the business takes priority in family members' actions, while the family side of the governance equation is under-recognized, underappreciated and underdeveloped. Family concerns then go unfulfilled — and grow potentially malignant — or surface in places where they don't belong, such as management or board meetings. Instead of a positive, the potentially powerful asset of family ownership can be converted to a negative, a drag on management and on business governance.

If the family is to survive, and its role as the capital base of the business with it, family members must develop a collective agenda, purpose, and methods for resolving differences.

III. *The Differing Roles of the Family and the Board*

The principle of parallel focus on the interests of family and business, in our experience, has proven the best and most enduring strategy for successful family businesses.

Every family business, no matter how large or small, has "the business of the family" and "the business of the business" that require a dual spotlight and a degree of separation. While the twain meet on many issues and must be coordinated in a planned and thoughtful way, independence and focus are also crucial in maximizing the potential contribution and richness of each. **Like yin and yang, family and business are equally important and require mutual respect and equal care.**

This requires some essential disciplines of focus and separation. **Family members must earn a voice in business governance by showing or developing qualifications that convey the right to be heard.** These qualifications are the province of the family to decide, but they might include such traits as excellence at one's vocation, flexibility in viewing issues and literacy in the language of the business. (Please see Table 1.)

While the opportunity to be heard in relation to the family is often more readily available than in the business, many families have implicit or explicit standards for voice in the family council. (Please see Table 2.)

The second discipline: Accountability to the family. The business in turn needs to be accountable to the family. Business leaders must respect the right of the family to be informed about the business and to guide certain overarching dimensions of its functioning. It also means major business decisions are guided by the family's goals for the business on such issues as family employment or shareholder liquidity.

The importance of independent governance processes. Setting up separate governance processes for the business and the family is the best way to develop these disciplines.

The distinct governance needs of the family are best served by family meetings or a family council (or similar family organization). Business governance needs are best served by an active board, preferably one with a majority of qualified independent directors. These two measures often represent a family business's most valuable efforts to sustain a healthy family and a healthy business.

Table 1:

A SAMPLING OF FAMILY QUALIFICATIONS FOR EARNING "VOICE" IN THE BUSINESS

1. **EXCELLENCE** at your vocation, from homemaking to investment banking. Excellence at any vocation requires hard work, high standards, expertise and education. Excellence earns respect.

2. **FLEXIBILITY** in your views of difficult issues. That means you have the ability and desire to listen to other points of view, an ability to empathize and an understanding that you aren't always right. Open-mindedness reduces defensiveness.

3. **LITERACY** in business language and the characteristics of your industry. Family members who are willing to hold themselves accountable to the business will learn how to interpret financial statements, judge competitors and keep up with business trends. Literacy eases communication.

4. **PREPAREDNESS** to understand business concerns. This means a willingness to do your homework and to study and understand the information you are given by management.

5. **TRUST** in management. Family members' trust in experienced, talented managers, makes it easier for management to institute constructive changes, innovate and take the risks necessary to running a successful business. The more trusting family shareholders are, the greater is their capacity to strengthen the business. Trust makes teamwork possible.

Family meetings can range from occasional informal talks over dinner to regular sessions of a family council. (For suggestions on organizing family meetings, please see **No. 2** of **The Family Business Leadership Series**, *Family Meetings: How to Build A Stronger Family and A Stronger Business.*)

Table 2: _____

A SAMPLING OF FAMILY QUALIFICATIONS FOR EARNING "VOICE" IN THE FAMILY

1. Disagrees without being emotional.
2. Contributes to the family and is not dependent on family resources for survival or luxury.
3. Earns and retains a modicum of respect from all family members.
4. Puts the needs of family before self.

Whatever form they take, family meetings allow airing of family concerns, the development of shared expectations and smooth decision-making around a variety of major family issues. These issues can include money matters, jobs or careers in the family business, education and training, succession questions and much more. Family meetings also provide an opportunity for family members to learn to respect the complexity of the business and the roles of managers and directors in running it. (Please see Table 3.)

Table 3: _____

BENEFITS OF HOLDING FAMILY MEETINGS

1. Building a Stronger Family
2. Building a Stronger Business
3. Planning for Future Ownership
4. Planning Family Participation
5. Managing Inherited Wealth
6. Opening Up the Succession Process
7. Preserving Family Tradition and History
8. Professionalizing the Business
9. Managing Relations Between the Family and the Board
10. Recognizing and Resolving Conflict

SOURCE: *Family Meetings: How to Build a Stronger Family and a Stronger Business*. **Family Business Leadership Series**, No. 2.

The benefits of an active board. Active boards are a proven family business resource, giving ready access to great experience and expertise and encouraging self-discipline and accountability. (Please see Table 4.) **Family businesses with active boards tend to have faster revenue growth, more disciplined business practices and more deliberate strategic planning processes,** according to the Arthur Andersen's *American Family Business Survey 1995.*

Family businesses with active boards also are best equipped to help management meet such shareholder concerns as improving the quality of strategy, setting and reviewing objectives and policies, aiding in management and director succession, helping evaluate key managers, and so on. (A full discussion of the benefits and organization of an active board is beyond the scope of this book. Both are discussed in depth in *Creating Effective Boards for Private Enterprises: Meeting the Challenges of Continuity and Competition* (by John L. Ward, Jossey-Bass Publishers, 1991).

Table 4:

TEN BENEFITS OF AN ACTIVE BOARD

1. Providing In-House Experience and Expertise
2. Encouraging Self-Discipline and Accountability in Management.
3. Providing a Sounding Board to Aid in Evaluating Business Owners' Ideas.
4. Offering Honest, Objective Opinions on Performance, Strategy, Compensation and Other Business Matters.
5. Assisting in Strategic Planning and Monitoring Implementation.
6. Offering Insight into Key People.
7. Asking Challenging, Penetrating Questions.
8. Giving Confidential and Empathetic Counsel.
9. Aiding Creative Thinking and Decisionmaking.
10. Enhancing Cooperative Relations with Constituents Including Employees, Suppliers, Customers and the Community at Large.

SOURCE: *Creating Effective Boards for Private Enterprises: Meeting the Challenges of Continuity and Competition* by John L. Ward (Jossey-Bass 1991).

How do the board and the family work together? Keeping in mind the three-circle model of governance, let's look at a fictitious example of how the distinct roles of family, directors and management might work in a well-governed family business facing a common kind of challenge.

Widget Co. is considering a major layoff or re-engineering. Technology has changed. Competitors have grown more aggressive and new competitors are emerging as industry boundaries weaken. Profit margins are under heavy pressure. If Widget Co. managers were operating in a vacuum, they might simply hand out pink slips and double up workloads on remaining employees.

But this family business has in place effective governance processes that provide added dimensions of depth and accountability to its decisionmaking.

What is the role of the family? Through the family meetings process, the Widget family has already determined its shared values and goals for the business and articulated them in written policies. In light of the pending layoff, family members discuss how employees should be treated before, during and after the layoff, in relation to the family's express value of maintaining respect for all stakeholders. When will employees be informed about the plans? Will efforts be made to help those losing jobs find new employment inside or outside the company? To what extent and for how long will employees be supported financially after the layoff? Should employees' families be supported as well? The family comes to consensus on these questions and, through a spokesperson, communicates its position to the board.

What is the role of the board? Widget's experienced independent directors, most of them CEOs of other family businesses (including two who have been through re-engineering), discuss the layoff plan from several perspectives. Are management's proposed decisions consistent with the family's values? Are business needs reconcilable with family desires to treat employees humanely? Or is compromise needed? If a compromise is made, will it defeat the purpose of the re-engineering? Directors also weigh underlying causes of the dilemma. How did the business get into this position? Has management properly identified the cause of the crisis? Is the business over- or under-reacting? Through meetings with the CEO, directors help guide and inform decisionmaking and provide a sounding board for managers. They assure that appropriate plans have been developed and regularly review management's efforts to do what they say they would do.

What is the role of management? Responsibility for deciding on and implementing any re-engineering that takes place is the responsibility of management. What consultant should be hired to help with the downsizing process? How many people should be laid off? From what part of the business?

This example shows how the roles of family, board and management are separate and distinct, yet complementary and mutually supportive. The family assures that the business's handling of the crisis is harmonious with its values and mission. The board

The roles of family, board and management are separate and distinct, yet complementary and mutually supportive.

ensures that shareholder interests are served and tries to help management make the best possible decisions, as well as foresee developments that could force a repeat of the upheaval. And management takes the operations, human-resources and systems steps necessary to implement the re-engineering efficiently and well.

Exhibit 2 provides an overview of the separate responsibilities of the family and the board, as well as a summary of major areas where they overlap.

Surmounting hurdles. "That's all sounds great," many business owners might say, "but you just don't understand the special situation in my family business."

Instituting effective governance processes does often require rethinking some assumptions about leadership. Here are some common hurdles business owners encounter:

Objection 1. "Giving family members a voice will force me to give up autonomy and control. That's unwise, because no one knows the business better than I do."

Holding family meetings doesn't mean that family business leaders abdicate leadership. Family governance still incorporates two separate roles — leadership and membership. Good leaders listen carefully to family members, remain open to their advice and concerns and try to respond thoughtfully and respectfully to their input. To accomplish that, they organize meetings or family councils. But the decisionmaking prerogative remains with the leader.

Establishing family meetings or a family council can actually strengthen family business leaders by informing them about family concerns before they erupt into disputes. In such situations, knowledge is power — and a well-informed leader is best-equipped to avert problems.

Objection 2. "Involving family members in governance will invite meddling by in-laws and other unwelcome sources of advice."

14

Providing a process for family members to air their concerns doesn't mean the CEO has to take any advice that is given. It only requires him or her to listen respectfully and respond in a constructive way. Over time, family members involved in regular, well-run family meetings learn what is appropriate advice and what isn't.

And don't ignore the powerful positive potential of this process: Allowing family members to air their ideas in a timely way can prevent their concerns from festering into a destructive internal cancer that can destroy both family and business.

Objection 3. "I don't want to share sensitive financial information."

The focus of family meetings is family topics, not a detailed report of the business's financial results. **In the long term, however, it is impossible to sustain family trust in the business without sharing information.** As the shareholder base matures and broadens, it is wise to share certain measures of business performance. To have confidence in the business, shareholders need to know about and understand its financial results, outlook and key strategic plans for the future. Without family trust, shareholder solidarity is also impossible, and the future of the business will eventually be undermined. At first, some family shareholders may need to be guided away from trying to participate in business decisions. But in the long term, the risks of keeping financial data secret are far greater.

Regarding the board, active, involved directors need to understand the business's financial performance in depth. Any effective board holds all such information in strict confidence. But directors must have financial data to help set goals and assess and improve the performance of the business. Sharing data is also a necessary step to professionalizing management.

Objection 4. "Getting family involved in governance will turn the business into a political free-for-all."

Setting up effective governance processes usually has the opposite effect. By helping family members reach and articulate consensus and develop smooth means of problem-solving, it can avert backroom deals and damaging conflict. Once family businesses make a positive transition to organized governance procedures, governance has a way of taking care of itself. This frees the family business leader from the need to constantly "put out fires."

Objection 5. "Our board is already composed of family members. Why do we need to have separate family meetings?"

EXHIBIT 2 ■■■■■■■■■■■■■■■■■■■■■■■■■

Family Enterprise Governance:
Responsibilities for Major Issues

P = Primary responsibility
C = Contributing responsibility

ISSUES	Family (Owners)	Board of Directors	Management
*Family values/mission/vision	P		
*Communication in the family	P		
*Family education	P		
*Family relations	P		
*Aiding troubled family members	P		
*Resolving family conflicts	P		
*Philanthropy	P	C	C
*Family employment	P	C	C
*Management succession	C	P	C
*Dividends/distributions	C	P	C
*Market for stock	C	P	
*Business strategy	C	P	C
*Business culture	C	C	P
*Business ethics	C	P	C
*Developing & implementing strategy		C	P
*Day-to-day operations			P
*Employee relations			P
*Compensation	C	C	P
*Ownership succession	P	C	
*Family/Business relations	P	P	C
*Board composition	P	P	
*Selection of directors	C	P	
*Election of directors	P		
*Review business performance	C	P	C
*Community relations	C	C	P

This arrangement may work in the very early stages of a family business, but it wastes a major opportunity to support the CEO and improve management as the business grows. It takes up board seats with family

members who are already connected to the business, preventing involvement by objective, experienced outside directors who can bring new perspective and depth to the business.

Packing the board with family members has another major drawback: It encourages a blurring of the boundaries between family and business issues, a problem that almost inevitably leads to neglect of family concerns. Leaders of the family have a special and distinct role to play in fostering family cohesiveness and cultivating the unique energy and insights that only a family can bring to business governance. **The family deserves its own governance process, and allowing board and family functions to merge usually prevents this from happening.**

Objection 6. "My family just doesn't operate that way."

If the family's goal is to build and maintain a successful, multi-generational business, they may have to make changes in the family's customary patterns of behavior. As the business evolves from entrepreneur to sibling team to cousins' ownership, dynamics and relationships should be reexamined rather than accepted.

IV. *Organizing the Family*

One of the best ways for a family in business to succeed through the generations is to anticipate future issues and talk about them as a family — *before* they become issues.

But which matters *are* the prerogative of the family to decide? Members of families in business together wear so many hats — as parents, CEOs, sons, daughters, grandchildren, directors, shareholders, managers, trustees and so on — that it can be difficult to identify the collective role of the family.

The purpose of this chapter is to clarify that role: To find consensus on matters where owners' wishes matter most, and to provide family members with a sense of identity and mission that transcends their role as owners of the business.

Family governance should focus on some or all of eight key areas of family concern:

1. Setting family policy, or agreements governing family behaviors, actions or decisions.

2. Articulating family vision and mission, or the motivating values and principles that help keep the family working together for the good of the family and the business.

3. Attending to family organization, or setting up a framework that enables the family to learn together, share decisions and communicate.

4. Setting family ownership policy, or family policy in relation to the business; these are the principles that guide the business culture, goals and capital allocation, and rights and responsibilities of shareholders.

5. Resolving conflicts within the family and providing methods for helping family members in need.

6. Fostering family education and information, or making sure family members of current and successor generations have the knowledge and understanding necessary to play their chosen business and family roles and to achieve shared goals.

7. Coordinating family civic, political and philanthropic roles, or managing the family's relationships with the outside world;

8. Ensuring family fun, or nurturing the relationships and shared experiences that provide glue for shared endeavors.

Some examples of family activities in pursuit of each of these goals are contained in Table 5. While no family could do all these activities, the list is designed to serve as a kind of "menu" for families seeking to improve governance.

Let's look at each of these dimensions of the family role in greater depth:

1. Setting family policy. Many families set policies to guide future decisions and actions in a variety of important areas. These typically involve such issues as: How will we govern ourselves? How will we resolve conflict? How will we respond to family members in need?

Some families agree to a family code of conduct. For example, family members might agree to support one another in public, to speak positively of one another to spouses and to avoid issuing ultimatums to each other.

The family should set guidelines for family representation in management of the business. How important is it for a family member to be chairman or CEO? To what extent should family members comprise the executive committee? The family also must plan for general family participation in the business. What opportunities will next-generation family members be offered in the business? What qualifications must they have? Should in-laws be included? How will family members be compensated? How should family titles and authority be determined? Should family members be permitted to hold summer jobs? What if a family member fails as an employee? A corollary question is, What career and performance incentives should be offered nonfamily managers? The family also must weigh plans for ownership succession.

Solving Problems Before They Arise

Family policy was a major part of the discussion when one Virginia business owner invited his two sons into his auto dealership. The father and sons, one the owner of a commercial real estate firm and the other an investment broker, held a year of meetings with a consultant to work out goals, responsibilities, the potential emotional problems of working with family members, division of duties, decisionmaking procedures and problem-solving methods.

With their spouses attending some of the sessions, the brothers avoided many stumbling blocks by airing concerns beforehand. Then, father and sons agreed to a mediation strategy that would enable family members to deal with any problems they did have "without getting personal," one of the sons says. Working through potential problems in this way, before they happen, often helps avoid problems completely.

19

Table 5: ―――――――――――――――――――

A SAMPLING OF FAMILY FUNCTIONS

Setting Family Policy
—Develop policy on family employment in the business
—Develop guidelines for family compensation
—Develop employment policy on nonfamily managers
—Determine philosophy of doing business
—Decide on principles of ownership succession
—Create family code of conduct
—Develop processes for resolving conflict
—Develop processes for family decisionmaking
—Decide role of business in supporting family goals
—Determine family role in helping needy members
—Decide on family linkage with the business
—Develop guidelines for family visibility in the
   business
—Build family cohesiveness
—Sustain family ownership
—Coordinate estate planning
—Development retirement or personal financial plan for
   business leader(s)
—Set leadership succession principles
—Establish ownership succession principles

Family Vision and Mission
—Encouraging positive family interest in the business
—Articulate family values
—Identify and articulate family goals
—Create family vision statement
—Develop family mission statement
—Write family values statement
—Decide role of family history in business
—Decide family philosophy of doing business
—Determine role of family goals in the business
—Maintain family teamwork and harmony
—Foster family commitment to the business

Family Organization
—Decide how to administer, coordinate and fund shared
   interests

Table 5: *continued*

—Create a family bank or office
—Set rules for family membership organization

Family Ownership Policy

—Clarify the rights and responsibilities of ownership
—Decide principles for business governance
—Set goals for performance of family investment
—Develop principles of corporate capital allocation,
    including appropriate dividend and reinvestment levels
—Clarify business goals
—Decide makeup of business board
—Participate in director selection
—Set principles governing shareholder liquidity,
    including share redemption and company loans
—Balance stakeholder interests
—Determine character and risk of corporate investment
    portfolio
—Determine role of business in supporting family goals
—Set ethical standards for the business
—Develop guidelines for publicity and community role
—Decide family role in management succession
—Decide family succession as directors
—Determine rules for share ownership and transference

Family Education and Information

—Foster good family communication
—Encourage education in general
—Educate the younger generation about family and
    business
—Cultivate family skills
—Determine family responsibility as business owners
—Prepare future generations for leadership
—Pass on family traditions
—Pass on family culture
—Pass on family values
—Pass on family vision
—Write family history
—Maintain family archives

Table 5: *continued*

Family Civic, Political and Philanthropic Roles

—Set guidelines for family visibility in the public
  domain
—Establish philanthropic principles and policies
—Determine family role in civic life
—Determine family role in political life

Family Fun

—Organize family social functions
—Back family projects
—Attend to shared interests
—Enjoy the rewards of working together

As the family gets larger, its leaders or members must decide how to govern themselves. Should a family council be formed? Is a separate leadership committee needed? Should in-laws be allowed to join the family council and how should family leaders be chosen? Should leaders be elected by branches of the family or at large?

Families also must decide how and to what extent business resources will be used to support family members' needs and personal development. If one family member has a talent unrelated to the business, such as rehabbing houses, for example, should the business finance her purchase of some houses for rehabilitation and resale? Should the business make loans to family members in need?

An important note: Questions like these sometimes overlap with the responsibilities of the board, as discussed in Chapter VI.

2. Articulating family vision and mission. Even at the earliest stages of the business, the family can begin to understand it as not just a vehicle for employing individual members, but as an opportunity to build something meaningful together and manifest the family's vision in the community. Many families find making an effort to articulate a family vision and mission can educate and inspire family members as well as drawing them together.

The family vision is the foundation for a cohesive, well-informed shareholder base. It sends a powerful message to the outside world, fostering optimism about the future of the business. It sets the tone for the business culture, helping managers develop a sense of purpose

22

and helping to recruit and motivate employees. It can even inspire trust among customers. One example of a family vision and mission statement is contained in Exhibit 3.

EXIBIT 3 ▉▉▉▉▉▉▉▉▉▉▉▉▉▉▉▉▉▉▉▉▉▉▉▉▉▉▉

One Family's Statement of Vision and Mission

VISION

To be a strong cohesive family whose core values encourage the development of competent, independent individuals who enjoy working together as a team to build strong families, enterprises and communities.

MISSION

To build a strong and enduring family organization that promotes and embodies the family's core values based on a four-pillar foundation of:

—family get-togethers
—education and development
—a sense of tradition in both family and business
—a commitment to giving back

Many families also develop statements of family values. A sampling of the kinds of values embraced by successful family businesses is contained in Exhibit 4.

EXIBIT 4 ▉▉▉▉▉▉▉▉▉▉▉▉▉▉▉▉▉▉▉▉▉▉▉▉▉▉▉

A Sampling of Values Embraced by Successful Business-Owning Families

Integrity	Work Ethic
Personal Growth, Risk-Taking	Producing -> Happiness
Add Value	Spirit of Enterprise
Trust	Long-Term View
Reputation and Heritage	Stewardship
Give Back	

---

3. Attending to family organization. Family organization can range from informal talks around the dinner table to a more structured family council or other governing group.

As the family grows, part of its organizational responsibility is differentiating between the functions of family leadership and family membership. Some families formalize this distinction by organizing councils or committees of family leaders or elders. These may be made up of elected members or the heads of various branches of the family. They may receive input informally or through meetings of the family membership. Family committees or task forces may also perform certain functions such as writing a family history or providing career counseling to family members.

Some growing families take the added step of setting up a mechanism for members of the younger generation to make their voices heard. Some families make third- and fourth-generation family managers part of a special task force. Others form "junior boards" of younger family members who weigh many of the same issues facing the business board, but without the weight of authority or responsibility.

In large families, several standing committees or task forces are possible, such as the following:
- Family council or coordinating/oversight board
- Family education and development
- Family employment and career planning
- Family traditions and history/archives
- Family philanthropy
- Family shareholder relations/liaison with business
- Family social activities/fun
- Family office or shared services

While no one family would have all these committees, different functions might be organized into different committees depending on family needs and family size. Each committee offers opportunities for family members to gain experience and provide leadership.

4. Fostering family education and information. The family is responsible for keeping members informed and preparing them for their future roles in the family and the business.

Business-owning families have a special opportunity to convey pride in the family's heritage and achievements and to give children a glimpse of the rewards and burdens of business ownership. Many families consciously teach values, the rights and responsibilities of ownership and a sense of stewardship to the next generation.

Family meetings give members a chance to develop such skills as

24

leadership, conflict resolution, speaking, teaching and running meetings. They also provide even the youngest family members a chance to learn the importance of listening, understanding each other's personal styles, logic and values and following up on results. Another family role is to encourage members to grasp the basics of management, including the functions of strategic, capital, estate and succession planning. They also need to understand the distinctions between the roles of family members, shareholders, directors and executives.

As the business grows, families need to understand the value of a transition to professional management.

As the business grows, families need to understand the value of a transition to professional management. Family meetings can help educate the family about the importance of nonfamily executives, the value of an outside board, improvements in financial reporting and planning, and other issues in this transition.

Family members need to understand the financial goals and tradeoffs involved in running a business: achieving growth, improving profitability, managing risk and providing payouts to owners. Every major business decision requires tradeoffs among them; you can't have more of one without giving up something of another. Ultimately, the family must endorse tradeoffs made by the business.

The family also needs to understand that there are multiple stakeholders in any business — employees, suppliers, customers and the community, as well as shareholders. It is the family's right and privilege to say that family is the first and foremost stakeholder in the business. But family members need to be aware of the impact such a decision has on other stakeholders and on the business as a whole.

Sam Johnson of Johnson's Wax has led family owners of the business to consensus on generosity to the community as a shared family value. The reason? Family members' children and grandchildren will live there. In this, the Johnson family is recognizing the interrelationship among stakeholders. **Some family businesses even make tradeoffs among stakeholders a part of an annual report to family members.**

Preserving family tradition and history is another part of family education. Presentations by older members, family history books, family scrapbooks and family trees all can help family members learn about themselves and the business and identify shared values and goals. By looking to the past, many families gain valuable resources for the future.

5. Setting family business policy. Another set of family responsibilities might be described as developing a family philosophy of doing business. This entails setting goals for the business, determining governance and liquidity principles and setting broad parameters under which the business should operate.

The family is responsible for gaining consensus on what it expects of the business. This means deciding overarching business objectives. Should growth, profitability, leverage, or dividends be emphasized? What level of risk, or leverage, is the family willing to support? No business can provide more of one goal without giving up one or more of the others. It is the role of the family to decide what importance to assign each and, with the help of the board, to understand and weigh the trade-offs that result.

In a related area, the principles guiding corporate funds allocation among stakeholders are the province of the family, too. To what extent should business capital be dedicated to business expansion? To rewarding employees? To serving customers? To meeting family needs? What kinds of liquidity programs should shareholders enjoy?

The family also outlines broad principles of governance. What is the role of the business in supporting family goals? What ethical standards should be adhered to by employees and owners?

Deciding the makeup of the board and family succession to board seats is the prerogative of voting family shareholders. How should the board be structured? What should be the balance between family and independent directors? What should be criteria for board service? How should the business handle the retirement of family directors and succession of younger family members to the board? When are next-generation family members eligible to serve on the board? What preparation or qualifications should they have?

The face the business and the family present to the world is also a family concern. Does the family want privacy or a low profile? What kind of business and family image does the family want to convey? Some families set policies against single-person feature stories or photos and require members to talk about the family as a team, for instance.

The family also needs to decide who should own the shares. Must shares remain in the family, perhaps passing only to direct descendants? Can shares be given to charities? At what ages should children control their shares, and what voting agreements are desired?

As in the case of family policy, family ownership policy is often a shared concern of the family and the board.

The role of active owners

Most business-owning families have direct ties with management through members who are employed in the business. However, some families that have no members working in the business have developed a special role that might be called "active ownership." These families have members who are vigilant in staying in touch with the business even though they are not employed in it.

In the most common example, a family member might be chairman of the board, even though he or she isn't a full-time employee. Designated family members might visit and walk around the business frequently, to be seen, involved and observant. They may work on occasional special projects. This provides an active, vigilant ownership presence that can afford the business the benefits of family ownership — a sense of a family's values and caring — without day-to-day family management.

This doesn't mean family members are entitled to overstep their bounds and interfere with management. It does mean they are sustaining family involvement through their presence and interest. One family, for instance, has defined three separate "active ownership" roles for three family members. One makes it his business to maintain comfortable relationships with key business managers including the CEO, and to stay in touch with the manager-succession process to assure that family goals and values are respected.

A second family member informs herself about business strategy, attending executive- and management-committee meetings and participating in strategic-planning retreats. Another concerns himself with the business culture, visiting the company's stores and store openings, chatting frequently with employees and taking part in awards banquets and other ceremonies. By staying in close touch, this family sustains the benefits of family ownership despite its absence from management.

6. Coordinating family civic, political and philanthropic roles. Business ownership often conveys a high profile in the community, whether family members choose it or not. **Many families find it helpful to reach consensus on managing the family's visibility.** Will the family as a whole play an active role in civic activities? If not, should individual members who choose to do so follow guidelines acceptable to the family?

Is there family agreement on particular political principles or goals? If so, do members want to take collective action or finance others who wish to do so? Or should family members be discouraged from political activity or encouraged to stress their independence from the family if they choose to run for office or back a particular cause?

What philanthropic causes does the family agree on? Who should oversee the family's philanthropic activities and what principles should guide its giving? How should the size and timing of donations be determined? Should donations be made privately or announced to the public? Should they be made with corporate or personal monies? These questions affect all family members, as well as the business, and if managed well can foster family pride, cohesiveness and commitment.

7. Ensuring family fun. Last but not least, **having fun together is the glue that can hold a family together even in the toughest times.** The simplest activities — annual reunions or social gatherings, family meetings at a resort or other vacation spot or family retreats — can spark a renewed awareness of the family as a treasure and a resource. The socializing that takes place at such events can strengthen relationships and foster better communication about business *and* family matters.

Some families purchase a farm, boat or resort condominium for the use of the entire family. Such shared investments in family fun can strengthen ties and build goodwill that will serve both the family and the business well.

Setting family priorities. No family can address all these roles simultaneously; some find setting a list of priorities works best.

When fourth-generation family owners of Cargill Inc., the world's largest agricultural commodity trading concern, first met in 1961 to set mutual goals, they were able, most importantly, to address sore spots of family history, including feelings among some members that wealth had been distributed unfairly in the past, according to *Cargill: Trading the World's Grain*, by Wayne G. Broehl (University Press of New England, Hanover, N.H., 1992).

Then, the family developed a list of priorities:
1. To have the "best management at the top," whether that meant naming family managers or not;
2. To maintain a fiduciary responsibility to employees;
3. To preserve family control;
4. To continue to retain earnings;
5. To make capital grow.

This family consensus formed the foundation for shareholder unity for a generation — and three subsequent decades of record company growth.

The Value of Outside Directors. It may be helpful to make an important point here about one role that we feel should *not* belong to the family, at least not exclusively:

The role of director.

Many family businesses follow the path of least resistance in this regard. They keep strategic planning and decision making "all in the family" by packing their board with shareholders. As mentioned above, we believe the ideal board consists of a majority, or at least a significant minority, of qualified, experienced, impartial outside directors effectively working together with family business leaders. We'll explore the reasons in the next chapter.

V. *Organizing the Board*

The potential contribution of the board in the private company is often underestimated by family business owners.

Some see it as a rubber stamp for management. Others view it as a necessary nuisance. Still others see it as a convenient way to channel directors' fees to family members.

But these views waste a tremendous opportunity to improve business governance. Many business owners who are committed to continuously improving their businesses and perpetuating family control say forming an active board of experienced outside directors is the best thing they have ever done.

Many business owners who are committed to continuously improving their businesses and perpetuating family control say forming an active board of experienced outside directors is the best thing they have ever done.

In the private-company environment, directors are free to play a uniquely helpful role as a resource to the business, especially to the CEO, and to the family. They may play a broad role in assisting management, monitoring the business's performance and reviewing corporate strategy, goals and policies.

Directors also can be valuable to the family by providing an example of shared decisionmaking and a model of informed, responsible business leadership. An essential role of the board is to prevent "disaffected owners" — unhappy shareholders. By maintaining an open attitude toward family members and helping keep them well-informed, directors can do much to foster family trust and confidence in the business.

Who Are the Best Directors? A majority (or at least a significant minority) of board slots should be reserved for a special kind of person — an experienced, objective, knowledgeable outsider, usually an active chief executive, who brings to the table background in the particular strategic issues facing the business, as well as sensitivity to the special concerns of family-owned businesses.

An effective director's only interest in the business is in seeing it grow stronger and endure. We have seen cases where family members who

An effective director's only interest in the business is in seeing it grow stronger and endure.

understand the true potential of an active board have voluntarily relinquished their seats to make room for experienced outside directors. In a truly unselfish move, one family-business shareholder told his relatives: "Look, I'm here on the board representing my branch of the family. But my sister-in-law can do that for all of us. My seat would be better held by someone with a lot more specific business experience in this industry. I'm resigning and I recommend we restructure the board to include a majority of qualified outside directors."

From the perspective of the board, there are two additional reasons not to pack it with family members. First, a family-dominated board tends to expand to an unwieldy size as the family expands. Second, while some family members may be deeply involved in the business and understand it thoroughly, all family members aren't likely to be as well-equipped to help govern the business.

Family members who are knowledgeable enough to help with business governance are available as a resource to business leaders anyway, in their capacity as managers or shareholders. The *only* way to tap fresh sources of expertise at relatively low cost — qualified and objective outsiders with great wisdom and deep industry knowledge — is through directorships.

One family or four families? The makeup of the board also sends subtle but powerful messages to family about the family's role in the business.

Naming directors from various branches of the family promotes factionalism. It suggests that the interests of members of different branches of the family are different, and that representatives of each branch must be present in order to make sure they are protected.

Outside, independent directors can be carefully selected so as not to represent particular branch interests. Instead, they represent and reinforce the notion of determining the best interests of the entire business and all its owners. It is usually more productive to view the family as *one family*, and to build on

It is usually more productive to view the family as **one family,** *and to build on common foundations rather than to stress the divisions among family members by recognizing them formally on the board.*

common foundations rather than to stress the divisions among family members by recognizing them formally on the board.

One successful business in its fourth generation of family ownership wrestled hard with the question of family succession on the board. Four brothers and sisters were considering their successors in their roles of directors and trustees. They were struggling to decide how those seats should be filled. All assumed that whatever arrangements they made should perpetuate equal representation on the board of each separate branch of the family.

As they debated the issue, a trusted adviser broke in with a question: "Are you one family or are you four families?"

After a silence, one family member responded, "We're one family, but we're acting as though we're four separate families." Their assumptions, they realized, merely increased the likelihood that other family members would behave in the future as if they were separate families. "We don't want to do that," these elders decided. And they proceeded to restructure the board in a way that would de-emphasize divisions among family branches and stress goals that united them.

Managing the transition to an active outside board. There is no substitute for beginning early to shape family members' expectations about the role and makeup of the board. **Involving outside directors in the first or second generation of family business ownership is far easier than reshaping an oversized fourth-generation board packed with representatives of every branch of the family.**

But if adding outside directors does involve separating family members from the board, it helps to communicate openly about needed changes and to emphasize the positive. The CEO might stress the added value outside directors can bring to the business and to the family's investment. Emphasizing the importance of the family council to the continuity of the business can alleviate family members' sense of loss, too. Having meaningful opportunities for involvement and impact by family members on a family council or other body (like the board of a family foundation) can ease transition strains.

Some family businesses ease the impact of a change to an outside board by phasing in independent directors over five to ten years. If family members are upset over losing directors' fees, the business might consider other forms of providing income.

One family-owned printing company managed this process especially well. Tensions over family compensation in the business and other issues led family members to realize that they needed the help of experienced outside directors. So the family decided to remake the board, which at twelve members was too big and was composed entirely of family. Eight family members would step down, the family decided, making room for three outsiders. Four family members including the chairman and the president of the company would retain seats. Two other family directors would be selected by family vote.

Candidates for the new outside director slots were chosen by the CEO and a consultant, then invited to meet with the family before selections were made. Family members' opinions were weighed in the final selections. In this fashion, the family decided the general makeup of the board and members' opinions influenced the selection of directors. But once the new board was in place, nominations and the actual choice of directors rested with the people most intimately familiar with the business's long-range strategic needs — its directors.

Throughout the process, the CEO stressed the positive potential value of outside directors to the business and the family. The opportunity to gain access to such experienced, expert people at a relatively low cost was especially appealing to shareholders.

Recruiting directors. Some business owners hesitate to form active boards because they don't know how to find qualified directors or fear that experienced people won't serve. Our experience clearly demonstrates that identifying and recruiting good directors is a very "do-able" task. Successful business leaders are often eager to "give back," stimulated by the challenge, and honored by the invitation to serve as an outside director. Though a full discussion of setting up a board is beyond the scope of this booklet, here is a framework:

1. Envision the board's role in the company. The family business leader should develop a statement of purpose for the board, including the overarching role that is planned.

2. Develop a list of criteria for directors. The best directors have experience analogous to the needs of the business. A company with eroding margins, for instance, might benefit from directors with experience in mature, hotly competitive industries. A business opening new markets overseas could be helped by a CEO already successfully established in the same regions. And in all cases, directors must be sensitive to the special needs of family business.

3. Plan the board's structure and meeting schedule. Prospective directors will want to know the planned makeup of the board and the time demands they can expect.

4. Prepare a board prospectus. This one- to three-page document is a recruiting and networking tool. It explains the purpose and goals of the board. It describes the qualities and capabilities the business owner is seeking in directors. And it should describe the planned structure of the board, director fees and anticipated time demands.

One business owner circulated a "Prospectus for Board of Directors" to several contacts, describing his ideal directors as "active business executives, risk-taking peers ... (with) integrity, honesty, courage of convictions, confidentiality, discretion and tact."

5. Ask for referrals. It is usually best to eliminate from consideration the first people who occur to you as director candidates — lawyers, bankers, friends, consultants, suppliers and customers. Instead, the CEO should aim to recruit risk-taking peers — fellow business owners, entrepreneurs and CEOs, preferably those who have already surmounted in their businesses many of the hurdles that still lie ahead for you. Our experience suggests other CEOs are very open to thoughtful, sincere requests from another business owner for board service.

People who know the business well — suppliers, customers, professional advisors (bankers, lawyers, accountants, consultants), friends and business contacts — can provide referrals to CEOs, entrepreneurs and business owners who have the kind of profit-making and leadership experience most business owners need. Circulate the prospectus to let them know your needs.

6. Write a letter of introduction. Include a brief statement of your purpose and plans, including the fact that you are interviewing a number of people as candidates and have in mind several criteria. Enclose a prospectus; it will serve as a job description. Follow up with a phone call to arrange a meeting, typically over lunch.

7. Meet with candidates and visit their businesses. At this stage, the CEO should talk about his or her needs and ask the candidate about relevant experience. Some business owners have a facilitator, such as a trusted advisor, accompany them at this stage.

8. Check other references. Seek out other people who know your candidates and cross-check their character, personality, experience and track record.

9. Assure shareholder support. Late in the selection process candidates should be asked to meet the family to provide shareholders an opportunity to make sure they are comfortable with them. Much like a jury-selection process, family leaders should have the right to veto candidates without going into detail about their reasons.

10. Make an offer. Finalists should share fundamental values, including integrity and confidentiality, and the chemistry has to be right, too.

Candidates also should display candor, an eagerness to learn and a lively interest in the business.

Once the CEO and the family are enthused about a choice, it is appropriate to do some "selling" to the candidate; most want to be persuaded, but it shouldn't be necessary to apply too much pressure to win acceptance.

Money, by the way, is rarely a key motivator. Directors' and the CEO's compensation should be comparable. If board service requires six days a year, pay directors what the CEO would make in six days.

The entire process may take several months to complete.

Some functions of the board. All corporate boards serve legal functions, approving changes to bylaws or articles of incorporation, approving mergers and acquisitions, declaring dividends and so on. A full description of these legal functions is beyond the scope of this booklet.

But generally, board functions should derive from five key roles: Ensuring effective governance; monitoring and improving business policy and strategy; providing advice and counsel to management; overseeing succession planning, and supporting family shareholders. Table 6 provides a sampling of activities in each of these categories.

Table 6:

A SAMPLING OF BOARD FUNCTIONS*

Ensuring Effective Governance

—Search for directors
—Select and evaluate directors
—Establish and review board mission statement
—Review corporate mission and philosophy statements
—Assess organizational culture
—Encourage family members to set effective governance processes.

Monitoring and Helping Improve Business Policy and Strategy

—Receive independent auditors' report
—Monitor business performance
—Review business goals
—Monitor business ethics
—Monitor debt/equity ratio
—Review and approve budget
—Review major capital expenditures
—Approve acquisitions, mergers

Table 6: *continued*

—Evaluate and approve strategic plan
—Challenge strategic assumptions
—Encourage strategic thinking
—Approve real estate transactions
—Approve officer compensation policy
—Ensure effective human resource planning
—Oversee litigation policy
—Monitor pending litigation
—Identify roadblocks to business performance
—Approve dividend actions
—Approve long-term loans
—Monitor risk management, including insurance
—Review accountability to stakeholders
—Review philanthropic policy
—Review company compensation and incentive systems

Providing Advice and Counsel to Management
—Advise the CEO
—Serve as a sounding board
—Help select executives
—Help evaluate executives
—Help evaluate outside advisors
—Encourage strategic thinking
—Provide in-house experience and expertise
—Provide self-discipline and accountability
—Ask challenging, penetrating questions
—Encourage creative thinking
—Help CEO clarify multiple roles

Overseeing Succession Planning
—Help plan management succession
—Help implement and oversee succession
—Help develop successors
—Plan and implement director succession

Supporting Family Shareholders
—Monitor shareholder liquidity plans
—Aid in successor development
—Aid in family education
—Assure adequate information flow to the family

Table 6: *continued* ─────────────────────────────

—Oversee family participation policy
—Monitor the strength of family consensus on business
   issues
—Encourage family members to reach consensus
—Build accountability and trust between active
   and inactive owners
—Help strengthen the business culture
—Aid in fostering a positive image in the community

*NOTE: This list is a sampling of board functions, not a comprehensive description.

Let's look at each of these dimensions of the board role in greater depth.

1. Ensuring effective governance. Directors play a major role in governance by helping ensure that the people and processes for orderly, effective decisionmaking are in place.

This means organizing a smooth search, selection and succession process for directors. It means setting and keeping up to date a meaningful and comprehensive mission for the board, and helping management do the same for the business. (One example of a board mission statement is contained in Exhibit 5.) An effective board also can assess the business culture and help management capitalize on strengths.

EXIBIT 5: ▐███████████████████████████████████████

One Business Board's Statement of Vision and Mission

VISION
To be a dynamic, enduring and successful family controlled holding company adding value to our subsidiaries and developing management excellence in the working members of the family and others which it employs.

MISSION
To build a leading and enduring diversified holding company which is based on a three-pillar foundation of:

   —a strong core operating company
   —a targeted group of higher risk venture capital investments
   —a diversified portfolio of income-producing securities

An effective board supports others in their effort to govern the business and the family well in several ways: By example, by speaking with family members and managers, or by mentoring the next generation.

2. Monitoring and helping improve business goals, policy and strategy. As discussed earlier, the family is responsible for determining the goals of the business in a broad sense. But it is the role of the board to review those goals and ensure that they are feasible and that the family understands the consequences and tradeoffs of the course they have chosen.

Monitoring the performance of the business is another role of the board. Directors can ensure that the performance measurements used are meaningful and that standards are applied systematically. And when performance falls short, board members can help identify roadblocks and figure out how to overcome them.

Another focus of the board is to help improve the quality of strategy. Evaluating and approving the business's strategic plan is one step in that direction. An effective board also can help the business owner challenge assumptions underlying strategy.

Directors also might help improve and coordinate business policies. That means reviewing the human resource, compensation, ethics, litigation, internal controls and other policies and practices and monitoring their implementation.

3. Providing advice and counsel to management. One of the most valuable and most often overlooked roles for experienced directors is to provide advice and counsel to management. Many family business CEOs feel isolated. Unable or unwilling to air sensitive management issues or to reveal their own doubts and fears to other family members or top managers, they may struggle to resolve them alone.

A good board serves as a trusted confidant, sounding board and resource in such situations. Also, family business leaders wear so many hats, as family member, manager and owner, that it is easy for their thinking to become clouded. Directors can help a CEO see which hat he or she should be wearing while deciding a particular issue. Good directors also are uniquely able to help the CEO select and evaluate key executives.

4. Overseeing succession planning. Directors can be a great help in getting started on a management succession plan and selecting the process for choosing a successor. Once plans are laid, oversight by the board helps keep the process healthy, deliberate and open. Directors can help mentor successor candidates and make suggestions for their development. And they lend credibility and authority to the succession process by ratifying the final choice. The board also manages succession and continuity of board positions, finding and proposing qualified outside candidates to the family.

5. Supporting family shareholders. The presence of an active, effective board is a resource to family members in several ways. Directors can help set and monitor shareholder liquidity policies, in accordance with goals set by the family. They can oversee implementation of policies governing family participation in the business and help evaluate family members' performance and compensation, certainly sensitive issues.

Respected directors are a resource for educating family members, both by example and by talking about family business issues in fireside chats, at family meetings or in other settings, as discussed in Chapter VII. The board also is a kind of insurance policy against crises — that is, if the owner-manager dies or is disabled before a successor is ready. In such cases, directors can serve as trusted advisors to a spouse or other family members, preventing hasty or ill-planned reactions.

Respected directors also can be a stabilizing influence on the family in times of high emotion or conflict, modelling problem-solving skills or discreetly urging resolution of the conflict. (Outside directors should usually avoid mediating or arbitrating family conflicts, however.)

Well-chosen outsiders command respect inside and outside the business, aiding in community relations. The existence of a respected board sends a message that the family cares about stewardship and is committed to the business.

VI. Managing Overlapping Concerns

A well-organized family and board, while focusing on their distinct responsibilities, also share broad areas of synergy.

As shown in Exhibit 2, many crucial family business issues are overlapping concerns of both the family and the board. Dividend policy, shareholder redemption policy, director search and evaluation, business goals, business ethics, family employment policy, and succession policies are among the matters that deserve both family and board consideration. In many cases, the family initiates decisionmaking and the board helps shape the outcome by helping the family weigh business consequences and tradeoffs.

In many cases, the family initiates decisionmaking and the board helps shape the outcome by helping the family weigh business consequences and tradeoffs.

For instance, the family might decide that it wants the business to pay high dividends. That is the family's right as shareholders.

However, the board might perform a family-education role by pointing out the consequences. Excessive dividends drain business capital and can prevent reinvestment or needed R&D spending, weakening the business and potentially destroying the family's economic foundation. When this message comes from independent directors, it may carry more weight than from a family member with a perceived vested interest.

Similarly, many family policy decisions require a clear and immediate understanding of their impact on the business. If the family decides to use business capital to finance entrepreneurial ventures by family members, for instance, the board must be involved in helping decide the interest rate, term of the loan and the degree of risk that is acceptable to the business. The family needs to be aware that such decisions also hurt the ability of business leaders to gauge the business's performance and assure earnings predictability.

In other cases, the board initiates the discussion. In searching for and selecting outside directors, for instance, it is the board's role to start the process and compile a slate of candidates. But the family has the right to respond and ensure its members are comfortable with the candidates.

To develop this kind of synergy, family and board must tackle these issues from a position of mutual confidence and trust.

What the Board Should Expect from the Family.

Directors can best serve those business-owning families who can speak with one voice, or at least who have made an honest effort to reach consensus on the family's vision, values and goals.

The family should be clear and consistent in communicating its goals to the board and others. This enables directors to be true to those objectives in their oversight of the business.

The board also should be able to expect individual family members to express in their daily lives the same values that the business is expected to practice. Any individual member's violation of family values — legal trouble or bad behavior in the community, for instance — can create tension in a business culture built on a foundation of integrity and self-responsibility, for instance.

> *Directors can best serve those business-owning families who can speak with one voice, or at least who have made an honest effort to reach consensus on the family's vision, values and goals.*

The family should be expected to do its homework — to read shared agendas, to educate members about family responsibilities and so on. And **directors should expect the family to cultivate respect for managers of the business, viewing them as professionals who play difficult and complex roles.**

What the Family Should Expect from the Board. Directors of family businesses are obligated to respect the rights, privileges, concerns and feelings of family owners. Owners of family businesses aren't usually dispassionate investors who see their holdings as just another stock. Typically, they are deeply invested emotionally in the image and performance of the business.

Family members should be afforded reasonable access to directors, as well as to information about the business. Directors should be attentive to family concerns and should communicate clearly and readily with the family.

Family members have a right to expect directors to adhere to the highest standards of professional evaluation of the company's strategy and performance — maintaining all the while a sensitivity to the fact that the business is family-owned. While this resembles the fiduciary responsibility borne by directors of any publicly held company, family business directors must be more attuned to how the family wants the business to be run and for what purposes.

While it's not always as easy to categorize the kinds of outcomes that business-owning families are looking for — a business strategy that will manifest family values in the community, respond to family desires for involvement or specific interests, foster initiative and pride in family members or enhance the family reputation — the family has a right to expect directors to show sensitivity to these issues.

Family members also are entitled to opportunities to identify with the business, to play a visible role at business events and to serve or support the business as ambassadors to the community. This might mean attending employee picnics or ceremonies honoring 25-year employees, representing the family at company-sponsored community events, and so on. Family members also should have an opportunity to tour new facilities.

VII. *Managing Communication Between Family and Board*

Several communication techniques have proven effective in helping the family and the board function smoothly and fostering trust and confidence between the two.

Planned linkages between the family and the board serve another purpose: Shaping younger family members' expectations about the board and deepening their understanding of the role of the family in relation to the board.

Having a family member serve as board chairman is a common way to link board and family, of course. Here are some other ways:

Fireside chats. Informal briefings or fireside chats give directors an opportunity to address the family informally about family business issues. These sessions can build trust and help shareholders understand the business.

In smaller families, one or two directors might meet with family members once or twice a year for casual talks. This gives them a chance to discuss ways for family and board to support each other. These sessions are also an excellent setting for talking about such issues as tradeoffs among stakeholders.

Written Communication. In some families, shareholders receive board agendas and minutes, as well as background on each director and information about his or her views. Some families send out periodic newsletters to update shareholders. In one family business, the board makes an annual written report to the family, including a discussion of tradeoffs among stakeholders. Directors also can benefit from receiving agendas and minutes from family meetings.

Annual social functions. Many families invite directors to attend all or part of annual family retreats, picnics or holiday parties. This provides an opportunity to get acquainted, share information and develop trust and open communication.

Joint meetings. Smaller families may gather family members with the board to meet jointly once or twice a year. This gives family members a chance to watch directors in action and to share and discuss family concerns together.

Regular requests by the board for agenda suggestions. Regular requests of the family for board agenda items, either from the board chairman or another designated liaison, signals a sincere effort by directors to respect and respond to family concerns.

Overlapping meetings. Other families plan meetings in a way that encourages interaction. Family meetings might be scheduled before board meetings, with a family member assigned to report to the board on ownership-related issues.

Special board sessions. Any time a major new plan, issue or shift in strategy is at hand, it may be advisable for the full board to meet with significant shareholders.

Family involvement in choosing directors. As discussed earlier, the family should be given an opportunity to meet director candidates and help determine their suitability.

Family observers or liaisons on the board. Many families designate one or two members of the family, chosen on a rotating basis, to sit in on board meetings regularly. Other families designate a person outside the family to act as a liaison. One family meets during a regular quarterly family meeting with its board liaison, a professional advisor, to hear a report on board actions and discuss them.

Governing committee. Some larger family businesses set up a governing committee of selected family members and directors to communicate and coordinate family and board concerns.

Directors serving as trustees for the family. Some families call on directors to serve as trustees for members of the younger generation — in cases where stock is put into trust, for example. This enables directors to manage the holdings with the best interests of both family and business in mind.

Directors serving as mentors to the family. Some families ask trusted directors to serve as resources to the family. This might entail mentoring a successor or other family member working in the business, but it also can mean supporting the entire family in managing family concerns. This director might attend family meetings and family functions as a resource, or make him or herself available to family members on a less formal basis.

Informal board meetings with shareholders. Some larger family businesses hold informal board sessions before or after the regular board meeting two to four times a year to discuss business concerns with significant shareholders.

Survey family members about their concerns. Some larger families conduct periodic confidential surveys of family members to identify issues and concerns. The results can be helpful to directors in understanding shareholder intentions and needs, as well as to family leaders.

*A **cautionary note:*** Even when such communication techniques are used, some family members still may want to take part in board meetings because they find them interesting and educational. Others might want to watch directors in action to make sure they can trust them.

While these desires are understandable, it is important that family members understand that if they do attend board meetings, their role is as observers. They should not expect to vote or participate in discussions. They should at most ask only an occasional question, and they should avoid leading the discussion off-track. In smaller families, a prescribed period might be set aside during board sessions for shareholder dialogue.

The key is to avoid diluting or diverting the special focus of the board. **Outside directors are special resources, and the more input they are able to give at board meetings, the more the family business gains.**

Family shareholders need to have confidence and trust in the board process. While family concerns are of fundamental importance to directors, family meetings or a family council are the best and most efficient ways to express them.

VIII. *How Governance Changes as the Family Business Evolves*

The functions of good family business governance stay pretty much the same as the family and the business grow.

What changes is the *form* these governance processes take. An entrepreneur and his or her nuclear family doesn't need to form a family council or junior board. However, three generations later, by the time the business has grown to a portfolio of companies and the family has expanded to several third-generation and a dozen or more fourth-generation members, effective governance requires a more formal framework to meet more complex needs. Exhibit 6 contains an overview of these changes.

EXIBIT 6: ▆▆▆▆▆▆▆▆▆▆▆▆▆▆▆▆▆▆▆▆▆

EVOLUTION OF FAMILY ENTERPRISE GOVERNANCE STRUCTURES

Stage	Family Organization	Coordinating Process or Mechanism	Board Organization
STAGE I: Owner-manager or entrepreneurial stage	Informal family meeting among nuclear family	Fireside chats or joint meetings	Ideally, outside board advisory council
STAGE II: Sibling partnership stage	Family meeting: Family members and spouses; sometimes, family council and/or task forces to handle projects	Fireside chats, joint meetings or governing committee	Board composed of majority of outside directors and selected family members
STAGE III: Cousin/ collaborative stage	Family-> family assembly-> shareowners subcommittees family council	Governing committee	Board-> Subsidiary boards Junior boards (as developmental tool)

The early stages. First-generation business owners often handle family issues in casual family talks around the dining-room table. At this stage, the family leadership and membership functions don't usually require formal organization. To aid in business governance, the business owner ideally would form an outside board or advisory council, a panel that performs many of the same advice-and-counsel functions as a board without the legal status of a board. Directors and family members might interact through fireside chats or joint meetings.

Though governance processes can be simple at this stage, understanding their functions is still crucial. In fact, family business leaders often need to be even more explicit about what they are doing *because* governance processes are so simple. The family business leader may need to point out, for instance, "You may notice that we've switched here from talking about what's for dessert to having a family meeting." Careful communication can drive home to family members at an early age the importance of good governance.

As children grow older, parents may spend more time talking with them about the business. Family participation, succession, leadership transition and family skill-building are often the focal points of these talks.

The sibling partnership stage. Many families start holding more formal family meetings after members of the second generation reach their 20s and beyond. Often, spouses of the second generation are included.

At this stage, questions about family participation and succession take center stage. Some families begin to rely on the help of a facilitator — a trusted consultant or advisor with experience in family meetings and an understanding of both the family and the business. A few form family councils at this stage, with larger families sometimes delegating special projects, such as a family-history project or family retreat, to task forces.

As second-generation family members assume larger roles, the focus often shifts to teambuilding, setting common goals and cultivating mutual interests, such as family harmony and family education. At this stage, many families find they need to be more explicit about shared goals and mutual interests. Some must make an effort to sustain family harmony. Family members may need educating, too, about any steps to professionalize management or revitalize strategy of the business.

The ideal board setup at this stage is usually an active board composed of a majority of outside directors and selected family members. The board and family typically interact through fireside chats, joint meetings or perhaps through a governing committee composed of both selected family members and directors.

Until the third generation of family ownership, or until the family reaches 10 or 15 members or more in size, most family-governance issues can be handled through family meetings, guided by agreed-upon family policies.

The cousin or collaborative stage. Family responsibilities in the third generation of family ownership and beyond become more complex. **As some family members grow more remote from management of the business, family concerns tend to focus more on shareholder issues, such as liquidity. A crucial role of the family at this stage is to foster a continuing sense of family identity and commitment to the business.** The family often naturally develops greater interest in family tradition and history, a valuable resource for strengthening the family and the culture of the business.

At this stage, the distinction between the family functions of membership and leadership usually should be formalized through separate family-membership and family-leadership organizations. Family members, for instance, may meet as a family association or membership group, often called a family assembly. If they haven't done so already, families must decide at this stage who can be members of the family association. Will in-laws be included? At what age may next-generation members join? Must new members of the family group go through some kind of educational process before joining?

The family association might in turn agree to delegate leadership responsibility to a separate panel. The leadership function might be served by a family council, family governing committee or family coordinating committee, perhaps made up of members elected by the family or chosen by a family leader. Some families create a leadership panel entirely of older-generation members and call it a council of elders. Others have a council of elders that plays an advisory role, helping the family adhere to shared values and traditions.

In one large family business, all 50 family members meet twice a year in a family assembly. But five people elected by that group comprise the family council, whose role is to provide guidance and set agendas for the family association, as well as making some decisions for the family as a whole. Other families create a family council made up only of family members who are employed in the business. (This isn't necessarily the best way to choose family leaders, because it ignores any special qualifications other family members may have to lead the family — vision, leadership or an ability to foster consensus, for example. Nevertheless, some families do use employment in the business as an organizing principle.)

Some family organizations write charters to specify the purposes of the organization, its makeup, meeting frequency, governance and plans to pay meeting expenses. Others are governed through a collection of family policies. Either way, questions about membership, rights and responsibilities of members, voting powers, selection of officers and other issues have to be decided. How will the operation of the association be financed? Should business or personal funds be used? Should the family organization pay members' travel expenses for meetings, finance family vacations together, and so on?

The first priority in any family meeting is for as many people to attend as possible, especially shareholders not employed in the family business.

The first priority in any family meeting is for as many people to attend as possible, especially shareholders not employed in the family business. That means that in larger families, the family business typically pays for rooms, transportation, and meals and child care during meetings. Family reunion parties, however, should probably be handled as a personal expense. That avoids the risk of creating a negative impression on other stakeholders in the company.

Some family associations also have standing committees. A family education committee might organize fireside chats or educational seminars for family members. A communication and information committee might publish a newsletter and arrange for sharing of board and family agendas. A governance committee might oversee governance processes and ensure that problem-solving policies are in place. A philanthropy committee might oversee the family business role in the community. And a family history committee might write a history and manage family archives.

Some families develop additional programs to manage shared interests, such as a family office to oversee family recreational property, education seminars or investment services. A family bank may develop a family venture capital fund to foster entrepreneurship. All these activities should carry out agreed-upon family goals.

Governance of the third-stage business. At this mature stage, the business may have evolved into a portfolio or holding-company structure. This might require a holding-company board, with subsidiary boards overseeing the performance of various business units. Some families establish family holding company boards made up of a combination of family members and directors, which serve as a linking mechanism for the family and separate boards of various subsidiaries. Subsidiary boards, in turn, are made up of qualified outside directors whose mission is to improve leadership and strategy in the operating companies and to support the top managers of those businesses.

Junior boards. Junior boards may be used at this stage as a developmental tool. These panels are usually made up of five or six younger family members serving two- or three-year terms. Members are sometimes selected on a rotating basis and sometimes automatically assigned to the junior board once they reach the age of, say, 25.

Often, the junior board meets right before or right after a regular board meeting in a simulated session. They go through the same agenda as the main business board and hear the same management presentations. With the guidance of the board chairman, a consultant or another family member, they listen to and discuss issues and think about what criteria to apply to decisionmaking. (Some families find guiding a junior board is a valuable and rewarding job for a retired CEO or chairman emeritus, who can pass on the benefit of a generation of business experience to future leaders of the business.) Most junior boards are not asked to vote on agenda items; discussion and presentations are used as learning tools instead.

By participating in these simulations, younger family members learn in depth about the judgment, tradeoffs and experience required of business leaders. If they meet before the main business board meeting, they may be given an opportunity to attend the regular board meeting and observe directors dealing with the same agenda. The junior board process can work nicely as a tool for including younger family members in the governance process and making them feel empowered. It also sends a message to the business that the next generation of family members is serious about governing the business well.

One business in its third generation of family ownership and management organized five fourth-generation members in their twenties into a junior board to consider succession and strategy. At first, members were confused and doubtful that they had any meaningful role to play. But with the help of thoughtful leadership, they weighed various roles in the business — from elders who were leaders of both the family and the business, to shareholders with and without voting power.

After discussion, they realized their primary role was in fact quite important: To influence decisionmakers by giving their input, and to learn about governance in preparation for the day when they would lead the family and the business.

The shareholder meeting. In larger families with more mature businesses, meetings of family members may overlap with shareholder meetings. This works fine as long as all family members are shareholders. If they are not, the family must decide whether immediate relatives of shareholders, or potential future shareholders, should be included in shareholder meetings. Some families invite spouses and other relatives to dinner before a shareholder meeting, or to a reception afterward, but exclude them from the business portions of the meeting.

It is important to remember, though, that the purposes of family meetings as we describe them here are far broader than those of shareholder meetings. In legal terms, the role of shareholder meetings is narrow, formal and restricted. For comparison, Table 7 contains sample agendas from shareholder meetings, family meetings and board meetings.

Table 7:

EXAMPLES OF AGENDA TOPICS FOR FAMILY BUSINESS MEETINGS

SAMPLE SHAREHOLDER MEETING TOPICS
—Elect directors
—Approve major transactions
—Change the corporate charter
—Approve selection of auditors
—Communicate financial results
—Interact with management

SAMPLE FAMILY MEETING TOPICS
—Family history update
—Family retreat plans
—Family development session: More effective listening
—Discussion of family values statement
—Presentation on family member pay and incentive plans
—Recognition of family member achievements
—Update on succession planning
—Report by philanthropy committee
—Family dinner

SAMPLE BOARD MEETING TOPICS
—Update on director search
—Review board mission statement and update if necessary
—Management report on financial results
—Update on strategic planning
—Discussion of proposed geographic expansion
—Review top-management performance appraisals
—Hear report from successor candidates
—Review minutes from latest family meeting

Table 7: *continued*

—Update on status of shareholder stock-redemption fund
—Discuss impact of planned acquisition on debt/equity ratio
—Status report on pending litigation

IX. *Summary*

Though governance is an abstract concept, the goals of good family business governance — smooth decisionmaking, cohesiveness, effective conflict resolution and freedom from political warfare — are necessary foundation stones to sustaining a healthy family and a healthy business.

Many business owners dismiss the consequences of failed governance — shareholder battles and defections, conflicts between managers and family members, or the destruction of the family by the business or vice versa — as the result of human failings or normal family-business tensions. In fact, these kinds of problems can often be eased or averted through effective governance.

Good governance means establishing two distinct and separate points of focus — one on the family, and one on the business. **The focus of family governance should be to find consensus on matters where owners' wishes matter most, as well as to provide family members with a shared sense of identity and mission that transcends their individual interests in the business.** That means attending to such shared concerns as family policy, or rules governing members' behavior and decisionmaking; family organization; family education and communication; the family philosophy of doing business; family goals for the business; family civic, political and philanthropic activities, and family fun. The best process for fulfilling these roles is holding family meetings or, in larger families, organizing a family council or other family association.

The focus of business governance should be to serve shareholders and other stakeholders and to meet the goals set for it by shareholders and management. The best process is to set up an active board, preferably including a majority of qualified, experienced outside directors. Such a board can provide advice and counsel to the CEO; help monitor the business's performance, planning and policies; aid succession planning, and help improve the quality of strategy. Directors also can support family shareholders, assisting in family education, monitoring family policies and helping build shareholder trust and confidence in the business.

A well-organized family and board also must manage overlapping concerns. Dividend policy, shareholder redemption policy, director search and evaluation, business goals and ethics, family employment policy and succession are among the matters that warrant both family and board consideration. In some cases, such as dividend policy, the family should initiate discussion and the board should review and respond to the family's decisions. In other cases, such as search for and evaluation of directors, the board should initiate decisionmaking, allowing the family to influence its choices.

Several communication techniques between family and board have proven effective, such as fireside chats with directors and family members, inclusion of directors in family social functions, or joint family-board governing committees. The family, in turn, might send a designated observer to board meetings or hold informal joint meetings with the board.

While the functions of good family business governance stay the same as the family and the business grow, the forms these governance processes take may change. As the business passes from the entrepreneurial stage through the second and third generations of family ownership and beyond, the family organization may evolve from informal talks over the dinner table to a family assembly guided by a governing body such as a family council. Similarly, the board may evolve from a single panel to a holding-company board with subsidiary boards overseeing various units of the family business portfolio.

While every family business is unique, embracing systematic governance processes can help any family business achieve goals shared by virtually all: Orderly decisionmaking, peaceful continuity and the freedom to make decisions based on the highest and best purposes of both the business — and the family.

Index

The Authors

Craig E. Aronoff, Ph.D., holds the Dinos Distinguished Chair of Private Enterprise and is a professor of management at Kennesaw State University in Marietta, Georgia. A nationally recognized expert on family business issues, he is a past president of the Family Firm Institute, an active consultant and a popular speaker.

Aronoff founded and directs the Family Business Forum, an educational program emulated by dozens of universities nationwide. He holds a Ph.D. in organizational communication from the University of Texas. He is author, co-author or co-editor of 20 books and numerous articles.

John L. Ward, Ph.D., is the Ralph Marotta Professor of Free Enterprise at Loyola University Chicago. A frequent speaker on family business topics, he has conducted numerous seminars and workshops throughout the U.S. and in seven foreign countries.

Widely published, Ward's *Keeping the Family Business Healthy* and *Creating Effective Boards for Private Enterprise* are leading books in the family business field. A noted consultant to family firms, Ward is himself an entrepreneur, partner in a successful real estate development company and co-owner of a retail hardware operation. He serves on the board of six family-owned businesses.

Over the past 15 years, together and separately, Drs. Aronoff and Ward have been recognized as leaders in the family business field. As founders and principals of the Family Business Consulting Group, they work with family businesses and speak to family business audiences throughout the world. Their books include *Contemporary Entrepreneurs,* first and second editions of the comprehensive *Family Business Sourcebook,* and the three-volume series *The Future of Private Enterprise.* They produce *The Family Business ADVISOR,* the only monthly newsletter for family firms.

The best information resources for business-owning families and their advisors

The Family Business Leadership Series
Concise guides dealing with the most pressing challenges and significant opportunities confronting family businesses.

Comprehensive — Readable — Thoroughly Practical

- *Family Business Succession: The Final Test of Greatness*
- *Family Meetings: How to Build a Stronger Family and a Stronger Business*
- *Another Kind of Hero: Preparing Successors for Leadership*
- *How Families Work Together*
- *Family Business Compensation*
- *How to Choose & Use Advisors: Getting the Best Professional Family Business Advice*
- *Financing Transitions: Managing Capital and Liquidity in the Family Business*
- *Family Business Governance: Maximizing Family and Business Potential*
- *Preparing Your Family Business for Strategic Change*
- New guides on critical issues published every six to twelve months

The Family Business ADVISOR
A monthly newsletter about successful business management, family relations and asset protection.

Family Business Sourcebook II
Edited by Drs. Aronoff and Ward, with Dr. Joseph H. Astrachan, *Family Business Sourcebook II* contains the best thoughts, advice, experience and insights on the subject of family business. Virtually all of the best-known experts in the field are represented — an essential addition to the libraries of professionals, researchers, students and those who work with family firms.

Now Available:
John Ward's Groundbreaking Family Business Classics
- *Keeping The Family Business Healthy*
- *Creating Effective Boards For Private Enterprise*

For more information:
Business Owner Resources, P.O. Box 4356, Marietta, GA 30061
Tel: 800-551-0633 or 770-425-6673

See reverse side for order form

ORDER FORM

Family Business Leadership Series

_____ copies, *Family Business Succession: The Final Test of Greatness*

_____ copies, *Family Meetings: How to Build a Stronger Family and a Stronger Business*

_____ copies, *Another Kind of Hero: Preparing Successors for Leadership*

_____ copies, *How Families Work Together*

_____ copies, *Family Business Compensation*

_____ copies, *How to Choose & Use Advisors: Getting the Best Professional*
               Family Business Advice

_____ copies, *Financing Transitions: Managing Capital & Liquidity in the Family Business*

_____ copies, *Family Business Governance: Maximizing Family and Business Potential*

_____ copies, *Preparing Your Family Business for Strategic Change*

_____ **Total** Leadership Series (Titles Above)

$_____ Cost (number of books x price - See chart at right)

$_____ $69.00 (each) Family Business Sourcebook II

$_____ $24.95 Keeping The Family Business Healthy

$_____ $30.95 Creating Effective Boards For Private Enterprise

$_____ **Subtotal**

$_____ $139.00* yearly, ***The Family Business ADVISOR***

$_____ **Total**

$_____ Georgia residents add 5% sales tax to **Total**

$_____ Add 7% Shipping to **Subtotal**

$_____ **Grand Total** (US dollars only)

*Add $15 U.S - Canada and Mexico / $30 U.S.-All other foreign.

LEADERSHIP SERIES Multi-Volume Discounts *(Any title combination)*	
1 booklet:	$14.95
2 - 9:	$13.50 ea.
10 - 24:	$12.00 ea.
25 - 49:	$10.50 ea.
50 - 99:	$9.00 ea.
100+:	$7.50 ea.

Check enclosed _____ credit card: MC _____ Visa _____ AMEX _____

Account No. _____ Expires _____

Signature _____

_____ **Please enter my standing order for_____ copies of each future volume in The Family Business Leadership Series. I will receive a 20% discount from the list price on these volumes.**

SHIP TO: Name _____

              Company _____ Tel: (_____) _____

              Address _____

              City _____ State _____ Zip _____

              County _____

Return this form to: Business Owner Resources; P.O. Box 4356; Marietta, Georgia 30061-4356

For fastest service, fax to 770-425-1776 or call 1-800-551-0633